Foundations for Life
-A guide for the youth-

Table of Content ‖

Introduction

A good foundation is necessary for you to succeed in life. If you would grow to be a successful person such as a teacher, an architect, an entrepreneur, a nurse, an engineer, a medical doctor or a writer, it all depends upon the foundation you would have at this young age. The people begging on the street or the so-called failures you see around were like you some years ago. They are failures because they made a mistake or did not have a good foundation. It is my belief that, you do not want to end up like one of them.

It is important to get a good foundation if you want to be a successful person. The time for such foundation is now and not tomorrow.

What then is a foundation? A foundation is a set of values, attitudes and education (training) you need in order to be successful in life. They are different foundations for different people in life. If you want to be a lawyer, you need a different kind of foundation from the one who wants to be a teacher.

In this book, I am looking at the general things you need to succeed in life at your youthful stage. These would include education, values and decisions you would make in life.

Life is very complex. If you are young, it is difficult for you to understand so many aspects of life. The successful men you see around became rich because of their foundation. So are the poor people you see around. A good foundation for your future begins at this stage in your life.

If you are in school or learning a trade, take it as part of the foundations of life.

Dedication

To the African youth, that you would grow into successful adults;

I pray that, you would have bright and fulfilling future.

Chapter 1

REQUIREMENTS FOR A SUCCESSFUL LIFE

Success is a very complex issue but let me simplify it as; achieving your goals in life. If you want to be a medical doctor or a nurse and you achieve it, you are deemed as successful. Sometimes, we say that, if you buy a car, build a house and marry a beautiful wife, you are deemed as successful. They are all part of it if they are your goals in life.

What you need to know is that, you cannot close your eyes and become successful. There are some things that you must do. You need to acquire certain attitudes, training and habits.

Your father or family cannot give you success like a gift. You must earn it yourself. The best your parent, family and society can do for you, is to provide the opportunities for you. The rest depends upon you.

That is, sometimes you would see a successful person but his child would be a school dropout or a thief. Sometimes you would see a poor woman who son would a medical doctor, a lecturer or a successful member of the society. Success depends on you alone. I have come across people who inherited businesses, estates and large assets but in a few years, they have ruined everything.

Success is not magic or simply saying I want to be successful and you would become one. You would need certain attitudes, and education.

Some of the requirements of success include the following:

1. Education

2. Discipline

3. Fear of God

4. Good character

5. Good relationship with parents

6. Respect for elders

7. Good friends

8. Good counselors/teachers and

9. Tolerance, co-oporation and Respect for Other people"s opinions

Let me briefly comment on education and the fear of God. The remaining requirements would be considered in the chapters to follow.

Education

Everyone needs education. You need to go to school to learn and acquire knowledge. This is because, knowledge is power. Knowledge has the power to make you successful. It gives you power to read and understand. Education gives you confidence to interact with people. It gives you the skills to build friendship with other successful people.

The ability to read and write is very important if you are to comfortably succeed in this modern world. Of course there are successful people around who can neither read nor write. That is true but you are different. You are living in different times. Your time requires that, you learn to read and write so that you are able to adequately operate certain basic items as mobile phones, laptops, write business proposals and above all, communicate in French or English or any of the international languages around.

It is important to learn that, reading and writing is best acquired through education. That is why it is important to go to school and take your studies serious. I know certain people, who travelled eight kilometers to school and back. Some crossed rivers and streams. Others also walked through forests. This goes to show you how important they took education to be.

There is another form of education, which you need to note. It is not about reading and writing or learning Chemistry and Biology. It is about learning certain good habits and characters, which are necessary for achieving a successful life. It includes learning habits such as greetings, respect for friends and elders, and respect for other people"s opinions.

This type of education is necessary because to be successful, you need not only to be able to read and write; you must also learn to greet elders, and do other things which the society expects all young persons to learn.

Discipline

Discipline refers to adhering to set rules and regulations even if they are inconvenient to you. Discipline calls for self-control, obedience, respect for authority in the right sense and the ability to order your life. For instance, if you plan to study for two hours every evening, and you are able to adhere to it even if you have to forgo a popular soccer match or a television series, you are deemed to be discipline.

There are two areas of discipline I would like to consider here. These are moral discipline and time discipline. Moral discipline has to do with overcoming temptation of compromising your values. Time discipline has to do with your ability to manage your activities with time frames you have set for yourself.

A disciplined person would always respect planned activities and time allocated for each programme. If in your private time-table you have allocated

30minutes for visitation every week, a disciplined person would not say the conversation is getting interesting so let me stay for another 30minutes. You would definitely excuse yourself.

If you want to be successful in life, you must be disciplined. This means that, you would have to attend all school classes even if it is raining or you are hungry.

Issues like laziness, bad company and easy going can prevent you from being disciplined. Remember that, discipline helps you to achieve your goals in life.

Fear of God

Remember that, *the fear of God is the beginning of wisdom*. We are advised that the fear of God is to move away from sin and other attitudes which are not good for your development. If you want to be successful in life, you need to know God and do what he teaches. Stay away from fornication, alcoholism, insults, hatred, bitterness, envy, and cheating. You must also stay away from habits and activities which do not enrich your life.

The fear of God teaches you to live a healthy life. It protects you from activities which are not helpful for your education. The fear of teaches you to protect your body from diseases. It teaches you to be a good person.

In order to be successful, you need the strength to stay away from all manners and characters which are not good for you.

Chapter 2

VALUES YOU NEED

Beyond your academic excellence, you would need some values to pave the way for you in life. These values are like an asphalt road in the real life. In school, you would need good values to get you along peacefully with your friends and tutors alike.

After leaving school, passing all your exams and getting your certificate, you would need these values to make you acceptable by the society, your parents and friends. What I am saying is that, ability to read and write, which you acquired in school through academic learning, is not enough. You would need to cultivate certain values. These values make you a whole person.

Why do you think employers don"t just select people based on your certificates and grades alones but requires that you come for an interview? There are many reasons for that, but one of the important reasons is that, they want to access your aptitudes and attitudes (values to work and relationship with colleagues). There are many people who get a job and are fired in no short a time.

An old man once asked me, "There are educated beautiful ladies around without husbands and, on the other hand, educated handsome men without wives. Do you know why?" "I said no." "In real life, your certificates are normally not enough" he responded. "It is your character which matters most", he added.

You need to know that, if your education is not backed by certain character traits, you may not succeed in life. That is why our religious leaders, elders and parents try to teach us certain values. These values include; humility, hard work, respect for one's self, elders, friends and everyone. Others are truthfulness, honesty, love, generosity, faithfulness, peacemaking, gentleness, perseverance, curiosity in your area of studies, goodness, forgiveness, dignity and trustworthy.

These values should be part of your life in all your undertaking. They are like diamonds, which set you apart from the lot. They make you unique. God, employers, and parents are proud of young persons with these values. If you are able to possess them, you would definitely be successful in life.

Some of the values explained;

Humility

Humility is good trait for all successful people. It refers to considering others better than you. Humility does not say you are better than everybody. It allows others to praise you instead of praising yourself. Humble people are not shy to praise others and accept their errors.

If someone is better than them, a humble person would admit it and learn. They do not claim to a master of everything. Humble people are likable by friends and parents alike. God blesses them in all they do. They do not boast. They do not look down on others.

Hard work

It is said that, "the heights reached by great men and kept, were not of a sudden flight but they whilst their friends slept, were toiling up in the night". Sometimes to succeed, you must work for long hours. It is like trying to pass your exams. You do not sleep long hours and expect to pass.

You would have to work hard. This means that, you sleep less, read more, go to private studies, and go for classes as well. People who work hard do not waste time on unnecessary things. They are serious, level headed and do not hangout with bad company. They plan their time well.

Showing Respect to elders and friends

It is important to value everyone. It is important to listen to your parent, elders, teachers and friends. Everyone has something to contribute to your life. Listen to every opinion. This does not mean you should take every opinion, because you reserve the right to make your own decisions.

By listening to them, even if you disagree with them, they would come to appreciate the fact that, you at least considered their opinion. It is important to respect everyone because wisdom is shared among all of us.

Being respectful does not mean that you are a coward or afraid of anyone. It is rather the opposite. By valuing other people means that, you have a big heart. You are prepared to listen and make your own decisions. So do not be worried about other people's opinion. Value them, listen to them and take the best out of them.

Truthfulness

A truthful person sees one plus one as two not as two and a half or three. If you see black say it is black not purple. If you see or hear white, say it is white not blue. If you do, you would earn the respect of friends, elders and parents. Liars and bad people would not like you but remember, if they are seeking the truth in a certain matter, they would come to you. Eventually you would earn the respect of lovers of truth and good people.

Sometimes it is difficult to tell the truth for fear of getting someone punished or dismissed from school. The consequences of the truth you are telling should not your concern. Everyone should be responsible for his actions. Your concern is to tell the truth. Remember that, by telling a lie, an innocent person could be punished.

Consider the wrongdoings, corruptions and other bad practices going on, if we are to tell ourselves the truth, Africa would have been a better place. Say it as it is. We all owe our school, community and nation the truth. It is a mark of successful people to tell the truth.

If the goods are worth GHC5, 000.00, why do you say it is worth GHC10, 000.00? By refusing to tell the truth, you may be causing your parents, and society money or somebody his freedom. Someone may be punished wrongfully because you refused to tell the truth.

Please remember that, one plus one, is equal to two and not two and half. If you tell the truth, however painful it is, you would win the trust of others. In this life, remember that, truth is more valuable than any amount of money. Truth could also save someone's life.

Honesty

Honest people are sincere, frank and candid. They do not do things in the darkness. They open up everything they do for people to see. They are transparent. They would not cheat you. If your parents give you food provisions for someone, an honest person would give all to the person without taking some.

An honest person makes everyone comfortable except bad people. An honest person is the one his friends are prepared to trust with money or valuable items to his care because they know that, you would not cheat them.

So, be sincere to your friends and parents. If you are sent to the market, and there is a surplus after shopping, when you get home, declare it to the ones who sent you.

Love

Remember that, "Love covers over a multitude of sins." It heals wounds, brings forgiveness and clears away all bitterness. Love does not know an enemy. It does not keep records of wrong doings. Love is not stupid. It is not naïve too. Love is everything. Love overcomes any obstacle. Love can cross over any mountain. It gives you the energy to achieve great things. Every successful person, blessed by God, has love in his heart.

This love is not the love of sex, or for a boyfriend or girlfriend or someone who has done something good to you. This love is love for someone because he is a human being. It is the love which says that, do not hate your brother; do not lie to him; do not steal from him; do not mislead him; and do no harm to any living thing.

When you come to accept someone for who he is and not because he is rich and powerful to help you, then we can say that, you love that person.

Generosity

It is important to give to the needy when you have some to spare. If you wish to be successful in life, you should leave to give to others. It is not proper to hoard your sugar, "gari", food, when others are hungry. Sometimes it is important to identify the needy in your dormitory, school and share what you have with them. Acts of kindness are necessary for you.

In this, let me sound a small note of caution. There are some people who are "parasites". They are always feeding on people. Even if they have, they would hide their provisions in order to take from you. Be careful of such people. Give only to the needy. Remember, that, being generous does not mean you should starve. Give when you can. Do not hoard and let your food go waste.

Peacemaking: Be a Peace Maker

Peace is an essential requirement for development. It is needed to provide you with continuous harmony so that you can plan your life, work and succeed. In your homes, schools and communities, peace is needed for you to prosper. If there is a disturbance in your school, you cannot study and pass your examinations. School properties would be destroyed and that would affect your studies and development.

You should love peace. You should also discourage any act, which would disturb the peace of your campus, home and society. This is because the absence of peace leads to disturbances and many criminal activities. Absence of peace could lead to the closure of schools, hospitals, and banks. Sometimes it could lead to conflicts.

Be among the first to talk about peace. When people talk of demonstrations, burning of properties, and the likes, talk of dialogue. If you cultivate the habit of peacemaking, you would be able to acquire the skills to survive in a work environment and in your community. Why fight when you can talk your way out of situations.

The fact that someone has accused you of a wrongdoing does not mean you should pick up a fight or insult the person. In our schools and homes, there are elders and procedures to report such matters to. As much as possible, seek peace in all situations. When confronted with a situation, ask yourself "would my actions bring, promote or maintain peace?" We all need peace.

Gentleness

Cultivate calmness. Do not rush into situations. Do not be in a hurry to speak or react. Let tenderness be in your nature. Always be tender and temperate in your actions. Being gentle does not mean you are timid. It means you are levelheaded and ready to think through issues.

Employers and the society are happy with gentle people. As a young person, remember that, hot-headedness and rashness would not take you far. Any success you think you can get from being "radical" would be short-lived.

You would make a lot of costly mistakes if you are rash in your actions. Gentle people are normally reasonable because they take time to think through issues. They are moderates who refuse to go to the extreme. Gentleness should be the mark of every lady and gentleman. Cultivate it.

Perseverance

Every successful person has some level of determination in his character. Sometimes, you would have to try three or even several times before succeeding. Perseverance means that, standing your grounds or pushing till you succeed.

Sometimes the topic being taught would be

difficult, perseverance would tell you not to give up till you understand it. It makes you stubborn in the right sense. It tells you not to give up easily. You are always pushing and finding ways of succeeding.

If you wish to succeed, you must persevere. You must not agree that, people say you cannot do it so you are giving up. Go forward. Work hard and success would be yours. You must persevere in the right areas. For example if you are a student, your perseverance should be in understanding your courses and studying to pass excellently. Do not persevere in bad things. Always persevere in good things like studying, helping a friend or your parents.

Let me say that, always look forward. Do not dwell on wrong doings of friends. Keep your eyes in your head and look forward. Concentrate on the good deeds you have planned to accomplish.

Curiosity in your area of studies

It is said, "curiosity kills the cat". That is correct, if you are curious in the wrong areas. For example, if you get curious about what your parents does on their marital bed, definitely you would die or if you get curious about why we advise you not to drink alcohol, you would surely die.

Your curiosity should be in the right areas. Your curiosity should be in the area of understanding your subject matter of study at school. If your teacher teaches you that; 1+1=2, and you get curious about it, it would help you to understand your subject matter better and thus pass your examinations.

Be curious as in a manner of understanding and learning about what is important to your life. If you are in school, your curiosity should be about posing questions to your tutors for better understanding of topics being taught at school. Do not accept everything you are taught at school without examining further. Learn to pose questions for better understanding.

Forgiveness

Learn to forgive. When we talk of forgiveness, we are talking about letting go the wrongs that, someone or some people have done to you. It does not pay to hold bitterness in your heart against someone. It is a burden. Let that person hold that burden. Forgive those who wrong you. Learn from their actions and move on.

It is important to understand that, forgiveness is a form of healing. It frees your mind from the pain those who have wronged you have caused you. Note that, forgiveness has a limit. If someone steals your mobile phone or a pair of shoes, take it back, forgive him but report him to the appropriate authorities.

God expects you to forgive. He also expects you to be wise. That is why I urge you to learn from the wrongs people have done to you.

Dignity

Be proud of yourself. Keep your head high. Do not let people look down on you because they have more money than you have or because people say they are more attractive. You are also beautiful in your own way. Dignity has to do with self-respect, and confidence in your abilities. A dignified person is truthful, and honorable in your endeavours.

If you wish to be successful, you must be confident of yourself. Be proud of yourself. Do not allow yourself to be measured by money, cars, a big house or any material thing. If you would be measured, allow yourself to be measured by your self-respect, honour and your values.

Do not tell a lie for food. Do not follow the masses because it is fashionable. Do not sell your conscience for material things. Hold your dignity in the face of trials, temptations and challenges. Always keep your composure.

Trustworthiness

The society needs people we can trust. When it comes to telling the truth, can you be trusted? If you speak, or promise something can we trust you to deliver it or honour your promise? There is a joke that, "some people if they ask you to look up you better look down..." This goes to show you that, such people are not trustworthy.

A trustworthy person is someone you can trust. He is someone you can rely on. Always, his 1+1=2. To be trustworthy means you would not promise what you cannot deliver. When you speak, it can be believed. Trustworthy people do not compromise on the truth. They are honest and reliable.

Independency of thought

Do not always follow people. You should learn to make your own decisions. Think through issues and decide whether it is good for you or not. Do not take an action because everybody is doing it. That is not a mark of people who wish to be successful.

If you are asked to join an action or do something, it is important to join on your own volition noting that, it is good for you. Use your mind. Do not make decisions out of emotions or act because of fear.

Take pride in using your willpower to decide on an action. Do not say something is white because everybody says it is. Ask yourself; is it white? Following the masses could have serious consequences for you because every individual is different.

Tolerance

Learn to appreciate other people's opinions even if you disagree with them. It is called tolerance. Everyone has a right to express his or her opinions. Give them that respect. It is sometimes difficult to accept other people's opinions when you strongly believe you are right. The point is that, as much as you believe you are right, so are they. It is said that, wisdom does not lie in on e person's head. So why don't you listen to others. For this reason, it is important to approach issues with an open mind. Everybody has an opinion so be broad-minded.

Chapter 3

RELATIONSHIP WITH PARENTS/ELDERS

Good parents know better. They love you enough to put you to school, provide for you, and make sacrifices for you. Parents are a shield of protection to you. They are also a source of wisdom and guidance in this life. Hold them dear. Respect every word they say to you. In matters of life, they are an encyclopedia of knowledge and experiences.

Often many of you make the mistake of seeing them as backward. The fact that, they cannot send a text message, or chat on "Whatsapp" or play on "Facebook" does not make them less wise. You ignore them at your own peril. Though in different dimensions, they have passed through all the stages of life and experiences you are encountering or yet to encounter.

In my experience and wisdom from which I am sharing with you, always remember the following;

1. Your parents have your interest at heart.

2. Respect everything they say to you. It does not mean they never make mistakes.

3. If you disagree with them, respectfully share your opinion with them.

4. Never disrespect them or say something that would hurt them.

5. Do not talk back to your parents.

6. Do not fight with your parents in public. You dishonor them. And since they are your shield in the society, you dishonor yourself by fighting with them.

7. Do not lie to your parents.

8. Do not look down on your parents. It was through their poverty or illiteracy that, they paid your fees and brought you up.

9. Do not speak ill of your parents to your friends.

10. Establish a bond of friendship with your parents.

11. Share your thoughts, emotions and experiences with your parents. It would make them know you better.

12. Always remember that, your parents are a shield of protection for you in this life.

13. Note that, your parents are your best friends

14. Be a helper to your parents. For instance during vacations or weekends, you should help in house cleaning or accompany them to the farm or to the market or workplace. It helps to strengthen the bond between you.

15. Never forget that, there is always something news to learn from your parents. The moment you deceive yourself that, there is nothing they can teach you, you begin to break the bond between you.

16. Parents have faults as all human beings have. Do not use it against them.

17. Do not argue angrily with your parents. Disagree with them in principle but do not go further.

18. It is a taboo to fight against your parents. If

you do, quickly seek other elders to intercede on your behalf.

19. Remember to respect other parents too. The danger is that, many of you respect only your biological parents. There is so much that other parents could teach you. Note that, your parents can not give you everything that you need in life. You need so much from other parents.

Chapter 4

FIRST THINGS FIRST

Time to Study

Remember that, "there is time for everything". There is time to play, time to learn, time to eat and time to sleep. You must take note of this. If you fail learn this, no matter how talented you are, you may confuse things and make your life miserable.

At this stage in your life, the first thing you need is to get education. That is why your parents and elders insist you go to school. If you fail to study, your friends would leave you behind in life.

These days, almost everything is linked to education. If you want to be a nurse, you need to go to school, pass your examinations and graduate. So it is for a medical doctor, teachers, administrators, engineers and surveyors.

Understand that, education is a solid foundation for a successful life. So as first things first, get education before thinking of anything else. Education can be giving at home and at school. The general source of education is through school. It is cheaper and elaborate to get education from school. As such, I strongly advise that, you go to school. Study hard and pass your examinations.

Plan your study

Going to school is not enough for you to pass your examination and gain a solid foothold in life. At school, you would need to plan your studies. In planning your studies, you would need a timetable. There are two types of timetables. The first is the official one given by the school to cover all school classes and activities.

The second timetable is the private one you prepare to cover your private studies and activities on campus and at home. It is absolutely important to get a private timetable. So get one. It would go a long way to help you plan your social and academic activities.

In order to plan your studies well, you need to list the following:

1. List all your social activities such as church and club meetings.

2. Note the times you need for cleaning your dormitories and school compound

3. Note the time for washing your clothes and beddings.

4. Make time for group studies and assignments.

5. Note visitation times (of parents).

6. Note time for siesta (daily).

7. Make time for visitations (of friends on friends on campus).

8. Note the time for mandatory school games such as inter-hall games.

9. Note that, you would have to allocate time for

each of these items by having a private time table.

SAMPLE PRIVATE SCHOOL TIMETABLE

Days	5:00 -6:00	6:00-7:30	Periods (Examples Of Subjects Taught That Day)	Siesta	Preps (Subjects To Study)	Before Bed
Monday	Cleaning of dormitory, school compound and bath-ing.	Morning devotion. It is important to go to the classroom right after morning devotion so that you can make time to briefly go through the subject for the morning/day	Selective Chemistry; Social Studies; Core Mathematics	It is a time for rest and noth-ing else.	Selective Chemistry; Social Studies; Core Mathematics	Park text and note books for the following day's lessons. Normally, the first subject is most important since you can park the rest after breakfast the next day...
Tuesday			Elective Physics; Elective mathematics; Elective biology		Elective Physics, Elective mathematics, Elective biology	
Wednes-day			Elective Biology; English Language; Pre-Tech		Elective Biology; English Language; Pre-Tech	
Thursday			Inter-Science; History; Geography		Inter-Science; History; Geography	
Friday			Government; Integrated Science; French		Government; Integrated Science; French	

SAMPLE WEEKEND TIMETABLE

DAYS	5:00 - 9:00	9:00 -To Lunch	After lunch – 4:00pm	Late After-noon to Evenings	9:00-10:00
SATURDAY	Cleaning, Washing	Rest, Visitations, Leisure time and refreshing period.	Study subjects you find it difficult to grasp during the course of the weeks lessons...	Visitation, Supper and Entertainment	Prepara-tion for Sunday; ironing etc.. before Bed
SUNDAY	Church Service	Rest, Visitations, Leisure time and refreshing period (clear your mind...	Study subjects you find it difficult to grasp during the course of the weeks lessons....	Visitation, Supper, Ironing of School Uniform	Prepara-tion for Monday (Revising Monday lessons before Bed.

NOTES

In the preparation of your private Timetable, note the following;

1. Give equal attention to all subjects

2. Assign more time to subjects, which are challenging to you.

3. If your school environment would allow, give room for group studies.

4. Arrange with tutors/students who have better grips on challenging subjects to help you.

SAMPLE OFFICIAL EXAMINATION TIMETABLE

(Timetable, was released 30 days before exams)

Day	Date	Morning	Afternoon	Evenings when exams has started: Revision Subjects
Monday	3.06.13	Elective physics (1st Paper)	Geography (2nd Paper)	Revise the next day"s subjects(ECONOMICS)
Tuesday	4.06.13	Economics (3rd Paper)	nil	ELECTIVE MATHEMATICS
Wednesday	05.06.13		Elective Mathematics (4th Paper)	INTER-SCIENCE/ HISTORY
Thursday	06.06.13	History (5th Paper)	Inter-Science (6th Paper)	GOVERNMENT
Friday	05.06.13		Government (7th Paper)	ENGLISG LANGUAGE
Saturday		nil	nil	ELECTIVE BIOLOGY
Sunday		nil	nil	ELECTIVE BIOLOGY
Monday		English Language (8th Paper)	Elective Biology (9th Paper)	PRE-TECHNICAL SKILLS
Tuesday		nil	Pre-Technical Skills (Last Paper)	----------

NOTES:

Before Examination

1. Study and prepare well for the examination.

2. Have enough rest before every paper. In other words, go to bed early.

3. When there are more free days, give more room for revision to subjects you find more challenging.

4. Since in our example above, you have 30 days to prepare for the examination and the number of subjects is 10, you should allocate 3 days of revision to each subject. Thus, 30days/10 subjects= 3 days.

5. Your revision should start with the last subject and end with the first. This is the bottom-up approach. The advantage of this approach is that, your revision ends with the 1st paper of the exam. In this way, it would still be fresh in your mind. Revise upcoming subjects as the exam starts. The private timetable below is based upon this method.

ORDER OF SUBJECT	SUBJECTS	DURATION
1st Revision Subject	Pre-Technical Skills	
2nd Revision Subject	Elective Biology	
3rd Revision Subject	English Language	
4th Revision Subject	Government	3 Days for each Paper. It is possible to revise two subjects per day as the circumstance may dictate.
5th Revision Subject	Inter-Science	
6th Revision Subject	History	
7th Revision Subject	Elective Mathematics	
8th Revision Subject	Economics	
9th Revision Subject	Geography	
10th Revision Subject	Elective Physics	

6. Go through mental and physical preparation before the paper. The night before the paper, get all your materials: pens, pencils and theirs in place. Early morning, get into the mood of thinking of nothing else but the paper you have that morning or day. It is not the time for bad memories or to remember "enemies". Examination days are special moments, requiring the best of memories and special concentration.

7. Be confident in what you have studied. Do not be "scared" by friends who have the habit of springing up new terminologies on the eve of examinations. There are enough questions for you to answer and pass very well, if only you attended classes and prepared well.

During the Examination

1. Be in the examination room 30minutes before time.

2. Do not panic in the exams room.

3. Be confident and trust in what you have studied.

4. As soon as you receive your question paper, read through all the questions.

5. Afterwards, spend some few minutes to choose which ones you wish to answer.

6. Allocate time for each question and work within the time frame. Do not spend all your time on a single question because your ""apor"" has dropped.

7. Do not attempt to answer the most difficult questions when there are easy ones. This is not the time to show off. When the results are finally in, they would ask who got an ""A"" or a "1" and not who answered the most difficult questions.

8. Work at your own pace. Do not rush through because you heard the invigilator shouting; ""thirty minutes gone"".

9. Even though it is important not to rush, it is equally important not to be as slow as the tortoise.

10. Read through all your answers before submitting your paper.

11. Even if you have not finished answering, it is advisable to spend about seven minutes to go over your answers.

After the examination

1. There is the temptation to brood over the questions you missed or errors you made during the exams. Avoid such traps. After the exams, close your mind from the paper and look forward to the next subject. A bad mood can affect you in the next subject

2. Your duty is to write the paper and it is that of the marker to mark the paper. Do not worry over what does not concern you.

3. Take a brief rest after school chores and start revising for the next subject.

Social life and studying

In order to succeed, you would have to create a healthy balance between your study life and social activities. We expect you to take your studies serious and pass your examinations. Yet, without a social life you may become queer. Some people have only three coordinates in school; from dormitory to dining hall to classroom. So, you need to take part in certain social activities like school entertainment, sports and a club.

This does not mean you should belong to all the social clubs in school or spend all your spare time visiting friends or making noise. Some people are carefree and if you are not cautioned, you can spare the whole school hours roaming about.

It would help a lot if you join a club or campus in addition to your religious activities and school entertainment sessions. The essence of a social life whilst on campus is to help you to pick values and manners, which are normally not covered by academic life. For example many of you may pick socialisation and communication skills from club activities.

Do not be a bookworm, join a club but always remember that, your primary aim at school is to learn and pass your examinations.

A note of caution here is that, do not let your social life get in the way of your studies. It would lead to disaster. It is safer to sacrifice time allocated for a social activity for studies than otherwise. Social life whilst in school is to be seen as something you do to help you pass your examinations or gain something to help you develop fully as complete young person. Some students learn public speaking, leadership skills, event organisation among others through their social clubs.

Learning

One of the first things you must learn when you are young is values such as respect, humility, good communication skills, and team playing. Back in my school days, there were some students we used to call, "I walk alone". They never socialize or even bother to talk to anybody. Greeting people was even a problem for them. Do not walk alone. Learn to greet friends and work in a team. One day, it would help you if you come to work in an organisation. It would also help you to find your path in the society and in life.

For the ladies, passing your examinations is not enough. You need to learn certain chores such as cooking, housekeeping and "home economics". Time has changed so boys, you should also learn some of these chores.

Do not forget to learn how to save. It is all about savings. You save to buy a car, build a house or to raise money to start your own business.

Chapter 5

SOCIAL MEDIA AND WHAT TO DO WHEN AT HOME

The home is rich learning grounds for you. You have your parents, pastors, elders and the whole society to learn from. The following are some key lessons you need to learn at home;

1. Table manners. For example, not talking whilst eating, the use of cutlery or eating together with colleagues.

2. You need to learn house cleaning such as clearing of bushes, and gardens and your rooms

3. You need to learn house cleaning in the kitchen.

4. You need to learn setting of table (dining)

5. Food preparation (cooking)

6. Washing and ironing of your parents clothes. Do not leave it to your sisters/ brothers. You would be amazed that, it is not that simple. Especially the ladies clothes.

7. Pick up a hobby such as knitting, painting, or...

8. Assisting your parents or guardians in their workplaces.

9. If available, you can pick a part time job to make some coins and kill off boredom.

10. Remember to study whilst at home. The fact that you are on vacation does not mean your books are on holidays.

11. Join your communities in communal works. You would learn something at these meetings.

12. Do not abandon your neighbourhood. Do not let them influence you negatively though. You would have to consult your

parents or guardians if you live in a rough neighbourhood. .

13. Spend as much time with your parents as possible. This is the time to ask them question about life, which bothers you. Your friends and strangers are not the people to ask for social advice from.

14. No matter how many house-helps your parents have, you must try and perform tasks such as washing your plates yourself.

15. Occasionally wash your parents' car, if they have. It would save them money and they would love you for that.

16. As much as possible, try to link up with friends from other schools and pick some school gossips from. In these days of smart phones and social media, you need not to always travel to link up with friends and colleagues.

17. Share your problems with your parents. No matter how difficult they are, try and find a way to.

18. Remember that, learning does not cease because you are on vacation. You only have to slow down a bit.

Sample timetable when at home:

Days	Morning	Afternoon	Evening	Bed
Monday	Reading	Help parents on the farm, office or on the market	At home with family to help in the kitchen or any chores required	Time for reflections and learning and social media
Tuesday	Reading			
Wednesday	Reading	Visitation		
Thursday	Reading	Reading		
Friday	Mosque	Visitation		
Saturday	House Cleaning/ Rest...			
Sunday	Church Service	Brief walk about the neighbourhood. (say 30 minutes)	Time with family	Time with parents for queries and consultations

You and Social Media

According to Wikipedia, "social media refers to interactions among people in which they create, share and /or exchange information and ideas in virtual communication networks". Note that, social media is not the platform for advice unless your parents or elders should choose to communicate with you through such media. Or unless you are communicating with a professional counselor you know. Consider social media as simply an avenue for meeting friends, sharing pictures and messages.

Learning could only occur on social media in a

controlled environment.

Social media platform is not the Bible, Quran or God. There is as much junk there more than you can imagine. The temptation is that, many of you consider what you read there as words from God. That is wrong. Crosscheck anything you read from social media with your parents.

Additionally, do not share your link with people you do not know. Many bad people now use social media to target young persons like you for sexual and abusive purposes. Thus many parents have begun advising you to stay away from social media.

I am not sure how successful those parents could be, because some of you have become so smart that, you register with false names, such as; lady brown, Beauty Queen II, Iron Boy, and Smart Daddy. How can I know that, my niece, Freda Boafo is the same as Lady Brown on social media?

Since you have grown smart to outwit your parents, my advice is that, use your real names and do not abuse social media or use it as a medium to replace your parents or our values. Not everything you read there is good for you. Remember, nothing can replace your parents in terms of love and advice.

You should also be careful it does not become a substitute for your books. It is infectious and or addictive. So regulate how many times you go on the platforms or how many minutes you spend on the sites.

When in school, it would not be bad at all to visit social medium platform once a week, on a weekend for a fifteen to a thirty-minute period. When at home, twice a week would be fine, for a thirty minute period on each visit is advisable.

Remember that, first things first. There would come a time when you can spend hours on social media; but this time in your life, is not that time.

Your main question on social media should be; is what I am doing helping me to learn something that would help me to pass my examination and be a better person? If social media is not helping you to learn something positive, then you would have to reconsider your accounts.

As I stated earlier, everything you do on a social media platform must help you to learn something new in areas of your academic work, manners and good character formation. Otherwise, social media would become a time waster.

Chapter 6

HABITS TO WATCH OUT AND RUN AWAY FROM

Life is very complex for you to understand when you are young. There are some things you must run away from as fast as Usain Bolt. These things are dangerous and can destroy you for life. Even adults tend to run away from them.

These include:

Bad friendship

It is said that, "bad friendship, corrupts good manners.." It is absolutely true that, if you join a bad company, they would give you advice or lead you into habits and appetites, which would destroy your life. Instead of leading you to study and pass examinations, they would mislead you from your books and you would definitely fail your exams and life.

At the onset, these friends would seem to be making you "smart". But eventually, they would lead you to failure. That is why parents, the Bible, and elders advise against making bad friends. Some parents would go as far as to "beat" you to prevent you from falling into the snare of bad friends. Bear with their emotions. It is out of love. They want to prevent you from making a fatal mistake, which would spell doom for you.

Avoid those who say you are a bookworm. Avoid those who tell you to disobey your parents and elders. Avoid friends who ask you to experiment with drugs, or sex. Stay away from friends who keep you in late outings. Stay away from friends who would want to take you to nightclubs. Know what you want in life and you would avoid bad friends.

Unnecessary Curiosity

Be curious when it comes to your books and studies. Do not be curious about such elements as drugs, sex and "high" life. This would lead you into experimentation and once you are hooked, that may be the end of your dreams. Drugs have never helped anybody. If they are good for you, why have the government banned them. Or why are you taking it in secret. It is a deception. So is early sex, and pornography (*My brother pastor Bismark Gyamfi has done a nice book on pornography, I urge you to get a copy*). Sex is good for matured/married people so why not wait for the right time. Remember, first things first. What you need now is education and not fun or dangerous experimentations. Remember they say that, "curiosity kills the cat".

Laziness

You must run away from lazy people. People who sleep all day and try to use "false" means to pass their examination are dangerous to you. Laziness robs you of your ability to achieve something for yourself on merit. There is no honour in cheating.

Neither is it a trait of successful people nor does it make you successful. So be careful to work hard. Idleness can kill you. It is said that, "the devil finds work for idle hands." Get some to do. You may read a book, write an essay, clean the house or do something meaningful. Do not sleep all day.

Envy, Bitterness and Jealousy

You can succeed if you work hard and build on your good manners. Do not be jealous about what someone has. You can also have one. Envy makes you bitter and puts you in sour mood. Bitterness can lead you to do stupid things. People have poisoned their own friends and even family members because of bitterness. It prevents you from concentrating on what you have to do to succeed.

Envy, bitterness and jealousy cannot help you to pass your examination or succeed in life. They only make you weak. They make you suspicious of everybody and everybody becomes suspicious of you. They are like magnet, which attracts bad friends and misfortune to you. Good people would discern your envy, bitterness or jealousy, would run away from you. This is because, someone who is bitter, jealous or envious can do anything stupid. So avoid people who envious and jealous. Do not be in their company.

Run from gossiping and too much talking

You are bound to gossip or reveal a secret if you are fond of talking too much. People who talk too much, always betray their friend's secret and their own. So is gossiping. If you gossip, you are bound to be embarrassed in the presence of your friends. Gossips lose good friends. They are always being questioned by friends on leaked secrets. What an embarrassment. Learn to keep your mouth close. Learn to hear something and not repeat it to anybody. Learn to listen more and talk less.

The Bible says that, a foolish person, even if he keeps his mouth close, he is regarded as a wise man. Cultivate the habit of thinking instead of talking.

Greed

Be satisfied with enough. There are some people who are never satisfied with what they have. Even if you give them the whole world, they would still want more. This is not a good habit. You would soon become the target of people because they would reckon that, if you are not checked, you would soon come after the little they have. Do not be greedy. Be content with what you have. Some people wants to have all the provisions in the school. They want to have all the best sandals at school. They want everything! This is not right.

Lies

A lie enslaves. It is disgraceful to lie. Your lies can get an innocent person into trouble and a guilty person to go free. It can cost you your honour and freedoms. Avoid people who lie.

You are said to be telling a lie if you withhold the truth, either by distorting facts, withholding part of the truth or refusing to speak at all in favour of the truth. Truth does not kill, so stop telling lies. A single lie, normally leads to many lies and eventually, you would get yourself into many trouble.

So do not start telling lies at all. Truth would save you but lies would enslave you. A lie could cost someone his life. It could also cost your parents and the nation. Do not only refuse to tell a lie, expose liars as well. Run from the company of lies.

Chapter 7

HAVE A VISION AND DREAM

(This chapter is largely culled from chapter 13 of my book: *The Dreams Of Our Youth*)

Above all else, have a dream. In order to be motivated to succeed, you need to have a dream. This dream serves as a motivation for your life. Successful people always have a purpose for their lives. They dreamt big and prepared for the dream.

As such, it is important to have a dream at this stage of life. Experience has taught me that, the dreams may vary a bit as you grow but it does not matter. It would serve its purpose. Have a dream and let the dreams motivate you to study to pass your examinations. Let the dreams energise you to overcome the temptations, which may come your way.

Please dream and dream big. But remember to work hard. In other words, dreaming big without hard work would make you a failure.

A dream is a vision of your life. It is an item of who or what you want to achieve in life.

In this light, you would need a vision statement to also guide you. A vision statement is;

"An aspirational description of what (you) would like to achieve or accomplish in the mid-term or long-term future. It is intended to serves as a clear guide for choosing current and future courses of action."

Dreams are sometimes like mirages. They turn beggars into kings, slaves into masters and the homeless into estate owners overnight. In the dream world, everything is great. There are neither tears nor sorrows. It is a world of perpetual bliss. A world of abundance, where there is neither scarcity nor disappointment. All is well. Peace and Happiness reigns. Within this bliss, you have hope, purpose and light to guide you as you pertain to the ideals of your lofty dreams.

These dreams drive you in your endeavours. They may be bold or moderate but remember, the bold dreams are the ones, which leave your footprints in history. Thus, "the glory and memories of men, belongs to those who follow their bold visions". Or as it is said, "fortune favours the bold". No dream is too big to be achieved. As long as your mind can conceive it, it can be achieved.

It is worth reiterating that, in the context of personal development, dreams are a source of motivation. They are useful in serving as guidelines in your psychological compass as you navigate through the harsh realities of life. It is always shouted that, you should "dream big". BIG is good. In the context of fostering motivation, it is useful to you.

You need to dream of a society better for all and work to achieve it. A place better for Libyan youth, Rwandan youth, South African, Congolese and the Tanzanian. A society not controlled by a few whether directly or by proxy; but controlled by all and for the good of all. A country, where the standard of wealth is neither measured by financial status nor by temporal power, but by highest moral values, vision, and purposefulness which have once created and sustained great empires and nations.

Without doubt, most of you wish to live a modest life; a decent house, a wife, a husband, a family and a car or alternative means. You aspire to live a dignified life in your country. It is the dream of many of you to be part of the society, wishing for the opportunity to develop yourself and to contribute to the national efforts. This is a basic dream, with sound elements of contentment and realism.

Therefore, as you dream and struggle on great visions, certain elements and values such as boldness, courage, single-mindedness, perseverance, endurance, firmness and steady-mindedness, should be part of your attitude and character. Thus, dreams alone do not survive in the real world. Without the right attitudes and balance, they would not grow beyond your nose and ego.

Dreams and Reality

Dreams and reality are not friends but always go hand in hand. Sometimes you get more than you dreamt for and at other times, you get less. Why this is so, is a complex mix of issues unrelated to the course and lure of this work. The thrust here is that, there should be an understanding that, there is a big difference between dreams and reality. Thus, dreams should largely be a guide.

Dreams should be the inspirational road map of your life's ambition; a motivator and a silent voice in the storms of life; a friend adding purpose and energy to your life.

A Dream goes against reality. It neither despairs nor accepts the failures of life. It is a platform for miracles and impossibilities; a friend who drives away fear, despair, failure and positions you, always, in the right light for you to receive success and fulfillment at the right times.

You must have dreams; dreams which would uplift you to the level of your aspirations so that you can contribute meaningfully to your personal development. Your dreams should challenge you to develop with a sense of purpose in life. Dream to be one of the few people who dare to break new grounds. Dream to be those rare citizens, who set the pace for their generations and posterity, upon whose visions the burden of their generation and the future lies.

Short Term, Medium and Long Term Dreams

For the purpose of clarity, let us consider dreams in terms of short- term, medium-term and lifetime. Short-term dreams are usually expected in less than a year or two. They could be synonymous to New Year's resolutions; semester grade goals or a month's resolution. The short-term dream should feed the medium term dreams. In other words, short-term goals serve as the foundation for medium term dreams and lifelong goals.

Medium term dreams are relatively between three to five years. They could be courtship leading to marriage and timelines for young professionals. They could also be business start-up goals. Or career progression goals.

The lifelong dreams are long term and stays with you until death. It is the ultimate dream that would be the essence of your life. What you would be remembered for.

It is worth noting that, short-term goals should feed medium term dreams and thus the long term dreams. They should neither be disjointed nor non-aligned. Short-term dreams should help you to achieve your medium-term dreams by providing you with the skills and opportunities needed for the medium-term dreams.

On the other hand, medium-term dreams should provide you with the skills, competences, opportunities and attitudes necessary for achieving your long-term dreams. The path from the short term, the medium to the lifelong dreams should be seamless. Each preceding stage should provide a platform for the next.

The Successful Youth

It is your right to dream to be successful in life. This success should not be solely determined by either material wealth or personal gain, but by how much you would give back to society. This is the greatest sacrificial story of all. And if you should dream to be the one "who gave all to the society", then you would truly be a successful person in the life of the society. You do not have to be a politician or a "huge" figure to give back to society. Your little would be enough for someone in the society.

Steps Towards your Dreams

At this stage, it is well assumed that, you have already aspired your dreams in your heart. Or for simplicity purposes, might have written them down in your journal or diary. The next proposed step is to make time to undertake some simple exercises as thus;

1. Write your dreams again on paper

2. Ask yourself or find out what it would take to achieve your dreams.

3. Ask yourself; what skills do I need in order to achieve my dreams?

4. What other resources do I need?

5. How do I acquire the skills and resources required to achieve my dreams?

6. Identify factors which would militate against you.

7. Find out; How do I avoid or overcome these mitigating factors?

8. Pause with an open mind and reflect on the questions and statements above

It is worth noting that, going through these eight (8) steps could take a year, two or even three. The waiting would be worth it if you are indeed to succeed. This is your future and life under consideration so be patient and pay attention to details.

What to do after question number eight (8).

a. Remember to write down the answers to these questions

b. Read over them a couple of times.

c. Note which ones require action. Prioritise the actions in order of magnitude. (you may consult a friend or counsellor)

d. Group the actions into timelines (one (1) – six (6) month, one year and three year periods)

9. Keep these solutions in mind

10. Revisit your dreams as in question 1.

11. Ask yourself: what is the first step?

12. Take the first step

13. Remind yourself of question 3.

14. Then work hard towards achieving the dreams.

These basic steps should be used as a guide rather than a rule.

Things to Do;

1. Work hard at school and be tough

2. Do not ignore the advice of counselors

3. Love your dreams and see them as achievable if you set your character right

4. Remember that; first things first.

5. Get a notebook and note down ideas, which comes to you concerning the dreams.

6. Only associate yourself with friends who would help you to study hard and pass your examinations

7. Engage only in activities, which you shall deem, as necessary in helping you achieve your dreams.

Things not to Do;

1. Daydreaming

2. Over-enthusiasm

3. Pressure from parents, friends and society

4. Bad advice

5. Inability to focus and be committed to hard work

6. Do not be arrogant or claim to know everything.

7. Avoid people who discourage you.

Above all, remember that, your first and foremost dream is to pass your examination in flying colours. Passing your examination and progressing to the next level of your learning is the first achievement.

Chapter 8

PERSONAL HYGIENE

Why Personal Hygiene

Personal hygiene is essential for personal, social, health, psychological or simply as a way of life. It is necessary in preventing illness and improving appearance. It also plays an important role in social acceptance and can either improve or get in the way of your reputation in social situations. Being clean and well presented makes you confident.

It is important to understand the importance of personal hygiene so that, you can make informed decisions about how to care for their health and appearance.

Some of you, especially the boys, are conscious of personal hygiene because it makes you more attractive to the opposite sex, for some of you too, it is because of the health issues associated with it.

As such, do not be ignorant of the need and methods of personal hygiene.

Personal hygiene refers to the cleaning and grooming of the body. In addition to improving appearance, personal hygiene is an important form of protection against disease and infections of all kinds.

In brief, personal hygiene means;

1. Washing your hands

2. Taking a bath twice daily

3. Taking care when you are handling food and storing food

4. Being careful not to cough or sneeze on others, by using a handkerchief to cover your mouth when sneezing.

5. Cleaning things that you touch

6. Brushing your teeth twice daily

7. Throw away tissues that might have germs on them into a bin.

8. Use protection when you might be at risk of catching some infections.

9. Cleaning things that you touch if you are unwell.

Body Odour (BO)

Body odour makes one very uncomfortable in public. It normally occurs after puberty. It is caused by a number of factors which are medical in nature. Usually the following can cause body odour in both young boys and girls;

1. Wastes excreted through the skin, such as metabolised alcohol.

2. The actions of bacteria that live on the skin and feed on dead skin cells and sweat.

3. Unwashed clothes, such as underwear and socks.

In order to manage body odour, it is important to do the following;

1. Change underwear regularly

2. Change clothes your close to your skin regularly since the collect germs from the body

3. Take regular baths. Twice daily is advisable

4. Refrain from wearing dirty clothes.

5. Wash your clothes regularly

6. Start to use deodorants (You can consult a doctor or a school counselor for advice)

Hand washing

Through our hands we can catch many infections when we put unwashed hands into our mouths. Others are caught when other people's dirty hands touch the food we eat. Hands should be washed thoroughly with clean soap and water. Sometimes use a brush if your fingernails are dirty. Additionally, dry your hands with something clean, such as paper towels or hot air dryers.

Note the following:

Wash your hands:

1. After using the toilet

2. Before making or eating food

3. After handling dogs or other animals

4. If you have been around someone who is coughing or has a cold.

RATIONALE FOR PERSONAL HYGIENE

Body Image

Body image influences self-esteem, confidence and motivation. People who dress well, with good teeth, well cut nails and are without body odour seem usually to have good body image. They tend to walk confidently among colleagues. On the other hand, those with body odour and poorly presented, normally have low self-esteem of themselves. They may sometimes even be depressed.

A good body image is necessary for your confidence. Do not be influenced by "perfect" images you see on television, newspapers and magazines. They are mostly not real. Remember the following though;

1. Simply follow personal hygiene practices and the society and your friends would accept you.

2. Your actions and the way you behave are more important to most people than the way you look. That is to say, good image is not everything, your character and attitudes are also critical.

3. Personal hygiene practices will help to keep you healthy, give you confidence and be pleasant for those around you.

Social Reasons

Nobody wants to be talked about as being "dirty", poorly dressed or being regarded as having bad personal hygienic practices. As such, one needs to ensure that, our bodies, clothes are clean and well presented. As such, try and project a positive image by keeping to strict personal hygiene practices.

Health Reasons

When you are advised to wash your hands before

eating or after visiting the toilets, they are all part of the practice of helping to keep you healthy.

Conditions such as head lice, cuts, brushing of teeth, bathing and disposal of used tissues should be taken seriously.

Psychological Issues

It is said that, "by being well-presented, clean and tidy, people can feel more confident, especially in social situations". Being well presented is said to raise your chances of succeeding either in school or social settings, because it makes you confident.

Areas to Focus On

Hair

Dirty head hair mostly affects your appearance and thus your social acceptability.

Bushy and Greasy hair: It is advisable to keep your hair well cut and washed regularly with shampoo. For the boys, keep your hair well shaved and brushed. For the girls if you are not allowed to perm it, then keep it well cut and washed regularly.

It is important not to apply too much grease to your hair. It may collect dust and as such required to wash it more than it is necessary.

Dandruff: If you suffer from dandruff, try the various shampoos available. In case it is serious, there are some medical treatments available that are not harmful to the skin. For the best option, it is important to consult a medical doctor.

Head lice: Head lice are highly contagious. If left unattended, the lice grow large enough that you can actually see them moving and the white eggs (nits) are also sometimes visible. The itching you experience can make you very uncomfortable. The best way to avoid persistent head lice is to wash your hair, leave a conditioner in and comb through with a fine toothcomb. Do this at least once a week.

Teeth and Mouth

Teeth: taking care of your teeth should be a serious exercise. A beautiful smile can get you fantastic friends, but if teeth are soiled or breath is smelly, it has an entirely different result. It can drive all your friends away and make you a laughing stock among friends. It can dampen your confidence.

Brush your teeth twice daily with a decent toothbrush, a fluoride based toothpaste in the morning and evening just before bed. You can also use an antibacterial mouthwash.

Avoid drinks such as tea, coffee and red wine, which are thought to stain them.

Smelly breath: Gum infection normally leads to bad breath. If you continue to have bad breath after brushing your teeth twice a day, you would have to consult a dentist for medical attention. This is because if left untreated, gum infection can spread and infect your gums.

It is advisable to visit the dentist regularly.

Areas Prone to Odour and Fungal Infection

According to medical professionals, "unpleasant smells and fungal infections are most commonly experienced in areas of the body that are warm and not often exposed to fresh air: the feet; the genitals and some of our sweat glands".

Smelly Feet: it is important to note that, the feet contain lots of sweat glands. As such if they are confined "in socks and shoes the sweat has nowhere to "evaporate" and the skin bacteria will, in effect, attack causing that pungent "cheesy" aroma".

Here are some measures you can take to minimise smelly feet:

1. Wash regularly and dry thoroughly with a soft towel and an anti-bacterial foot powder or a baby talc

2. Allow feet to air when feasible and wear open shoes as much as possible

3. Change socks more than once a day if needed and make sure they are cotton or other breathable fabric

Athlete"s foot: Athlete"s foot is a fungal infection that causes itching, flaky skin and sometimes a sore, red rash. It"s highly contagious and can be unsightly. As such, it is important to go for medical attention.

Genital Areas: Genital areas can be prone to bacterial infections and unpleasant aromas if not kept clean. Conversely though, too much cleaning with scented products or soaps can cause thrush - a bacterial infection. The best hygiene for all the genital areas is to clean once or twice a day using mild soap and water. Refrain from using "wayside" medication.

Personal Hygiene for Young Ladies

Besides normal habits such as cutting of finger nails, brushing of hair, cleaning of teeth among others, there are key activities ladies should take note of.

The vagina is able to clean itself no special care is needed, other than washing the external genitals. Do not put anything like douches into the vagina, as the delicate skin can be damaged. Here are some personal hygiene suggestions for women:

Menstruation: Wash your body, including your genital area, twice daily. Change tampons and sanitary napkins regularly, at least four to five times a day. Always wash your hands before and after handling a pad. Note to dispose pads properly after use.

Thrush: Some soaps and detergents can irritate the skin of the vagina, and make thrush infections more likely. Some people find that they often get thrush when they use antibiotics. Use mild soap and unperfumed toilet paper. Avoid tight, synthetic underwear. Try cotton underwear, and change regularly. There is medical treatment for thrush, so talk to your doctor or pharmacist.

Personal Hygiene for Boys

It is important to clean the scrotal area thoroughly during bathing. Bathing twice a day is most recommended. Do not attempt to use any unprescribed medication for the private parts.

Failure to clean this area properly will result in the collection of bacteria which may cause bad odour and subsequent infections. The penis should be cleaned on the outside only.

It is advisable to wear loose fitting cotton underwear to reduce the chance of perspiration build up and subsequent aromas. Be careful not to "apply aftershaves or deodorants directly to the genital area".

Hand washing should be a part of genital hygiene as hands should be washed after using the toilet, and should be taught to children to become part of everyday routine.

Chapter 9

SAVINGS AND INVESTMENT TIPS FOR YOUNG PERSONS

Savings is a habit which every young person should cultivate. It cannot be picked up by the roadside. You would have to learn it, practice it and adhere to the basic principle it requires. The habit of savings if learnt at a young age in life, would become a major asset to you when you grow. We save to buy book, a car, a house and any other thing you may need.

Additionally, you save money to build capital to start a business. Many successful people I have spoken to in writing this book indicate to me that, the habit of saving money helped them in so many ways in their lives. It helped them in times of financial difficulties among others.

The concept of Savings

"Savings is the portion of income not spent on current expenditures. Because a person does not know what will happen in the future, money should be saved to pay for unexpected events or emergencies. Without savings, unexpected events can become large financial burdens. Therefore, savings helps an individual or family become financially secure. Money can also be saved to purchase expensive items that are too costly to buy with monthly income. Buying a new camera, purchasing an automobile, or paying for a vacation can all be accomplished by saving a portion of income."

Importance of Saving

1. Keeps your money safe

2. Earn interest if you save with a bank

3. Makes you prepared for surprise expenses

4. Helps you afford planned and large purchases

5. Achieve major goals you need money to achieve. Example books, bicycle and so many others.

Where can I save my money?

1. Banks. When you save with a bank, a savings account is preferable.

2. Credit union

3. With Parents

4. Saving box

5. Lockers.

6. Your carry bag

7. Pencil cases

Sources of money for savings

1. Money you earn from part time jobs

2. Gifts from parents

3. Weekly food and other allowances

Principles

1. Make it a habit to save surplus money

2. Spend within your means

3. Do not borrow money from friends unless it is absolutely necessary.

4. Always plan you expenditure. Make a budget.

5. Do not follow the crowd in your expenditures. His leads to buying items you do not need.

6. Be modest in your taste and material needs.

7. Do not associate yourself with people who spend beyond their means.

8. Buy items you actually need.

9. If possible, share with others. Or pool resources together to share the financial burdens. Example you can share the cost of a television set with your roommate, other than buying it alone, if buying it alone would a strain on your budget.

10. Avoid Impulse buying and learn to exercise self-control.

11. Know where your money goes.

Challenges to Savings

1. Following the crowd.

2. Spending without plan.

3. Financial indiscipline.

4. Bad influences from friends

5. Lack of or refusing to consult elders on intended expenditures.

Investment

According to Investopedia investment is: "The act of committing money or capital to an endeavour with the expectation of obtaining an additional income or profit." In everyday sense, investment is a form of savings. The simple difference is that, with investment, you are putting your money to "work" for you in a venture. You earnings are not fixed. It varies with profit accrued from the investment.

Other comments on investment;

"An asset or item that is purchased with the hope that it will generate income or appreciate in the future."

"In an economic sense, an investment is the purchase of goods that are not consumed today but are used in the future to create wealth."

"In finance, an investment is a monetary asset purchased with the idea that the asset will provide income in the future or appreciate and be sold at a higher price."

Sometimes, you could save money and use it to invest into a business venture or an activity with the hope of future returns which are of higher value than the initial funds invested.

It is important to note that, on many occasions, savings and investment go hand in hand.

Investment Tips for young persons

1. Get Education or skills: This is the first and most important investment you could ever make in life.

2. Invest in growing or polishing your talents.

3. Plan for your retirement as soon as you start work and begin to save.

4. Be prepared to take calculated risk.

5. Invest in proven sectors. E.g. the real estate

and energy sectors give healthy returns in emerging markets.

6. Consult investment advisors when necessary.

7. Make investment decisions based upon data and research and not on a hunch.

NOTE: for further reading, get copies of my books;

1. **The Dreams Of Our Youth**

2. **The African Youth Question, Issues, Actors & Solutions**

(Both Available From Amazon)

www.ingramcontent.com/pod-product-compliance
Lightning Source LLC
Chambersburg PA
CBHW050419290526
45786CB00003B/1330